Love it, love it, love it!

I have been out in this crazy dating market for the last several years. You have no idea the madness I've experienced.

People date, but do not ask the right questions when looking for a partner.

They get caught up in the emotional aspects and forget about the practical aspects as well as how they or a potential partner were raised.

I've noticed that people do not know what to ask either until things come up. You can't predict everything, but a lot can be covered in advance.

Don't wait to ask the right questions until it is too late because you're already deeply involved in the wrong relationship.

S. Johannes

Marriage After Retirement:

25 Questions to Ask and Answer Before You Marry

Free Audio Version Included

Amy Rose Herrick

Profit-Building Specialist

International Best-Selling Author

Published by Amy Rose Herrick

Herrick, Amy Rose

Marriage After Retirement: 25 Questions to Ask and Answer Before You Marry

First edition

Christiansted, US Virgin Islands: Amy Rose Herrick, 2024

xiv, 92 pages, 9 inches

Relationships | Marriage |Finances | Compatibility | Insurance | Estate Planning |Medical | Household |Religious

978-1-960427-07-6

2023940105

306.764

Amy Rose Herrick's books may be purchased in bulk for premiums, groups, educational, business or sales promotional use. For information, please write to: Amy@AmyRoseHerrick.com.

DEDICATION

To My Past and Present Clients,

Thank you for sharing so many real-life experiences with me over the decades while we worked through all the financial issues.

We enjoyed the easy, joyful, celebration times and we journeyed together through the expected and unexpected tough times too.

It is a privilege and an honor for me to be entrusted with helping you to navigate the financial parts of your lives.

May your relationship that you are building today be one filled with joy, happiness, great memories and be long lasting.

CONTENTS

CHAPTER	PG #

To access your free audio version,
please use this link:

https://www.moneywithamyaudiob
ooks.com/marriage-after-
retirement-q-a

INTRODUCTION

In case you are wondering, no, I am not an expert on relationships. What I can share with you and the reason for penning this title is an extraordinarily strong conviction, from experience, that your relationship with a partner will be the foundational building blocks for everything else in your life. Your long-term relationship with a romantic partner definitely comes into play on all the financial work I do with couples and entrepreneurs.

I will share I am in my second marriage. We have been working at this union for over 40 years so far and are still learning how to navigate new chapters of change every year.

Dating, courtship, hooking up, finding a mate or whatever you choose to call the selection process for a life mate is not the same day-to-day relationship that a long-term romantic relationship may evolve into over a lifetime.

Unfortunately, for most of us, good looks, slim figures, great hair, perfect teeth, our best manners, endless energy, and even taunt muscles only last so long.

Wealth and health can change suddenly, for the better or for the worst.

No matter how much you seek after it or how powerfully it pulls your heartstrings, love is often not powerful enough to conquer every emotional or relationship-related issue.

Some relationships fail to be long-term with or without marriage certificates.

Hopeful promises were made, and future dreams were shared before they ended with some promises that could not be kept or dreams that could be fully realized.

By reading this book and being willing to ask, answer, and discuss the tough questions before you are deeply committed to a potential relationship, you are showing that you are looking for tools to be successful in what, for some, has been an elusive desire: a long-term loving relationship.

It takes courage to complete these exercises. It takes courage to tell the truth about how you really feel about an issue when you do not know how the other person feels about your answers.

It takes courage to listen to every word spoken, to understand how another person you are thinking about spending your life with feels about the same topic, especially when you disagree.

These short, thought-provoking questions were created to help you as a couple to talk through the issues that, if left unchecked, could destroy your relationship over time.

Each question has space for each of you to write your thoughts if you choose to. Some questions may sound silly to you in the context of your life experience.

Some may make you laugh.

Some answers given by your partner could upset you.

Other answers could result in the assurance you are both in total agreement on the topic. Ask!

Listening is the key.

Do not get distracted formulating your response while the other person is still talking. You cannot listen and formulate a response at the same time.

Be realistic.

If your partner is 100% passionate about an issue and you are barely 5%, can you be supportive and do it their way with ease?

Will your chosen one give you the support you need to proceed on an issue your way when you are 80% enthusiastic about choice "A" and they are 50% to go either way when choices "A" & "B" are very different?

Will you meet somewhere in the middle that is agreeable to both of you? Do you intend to really do your best trying to compromise as conflicts arise? Do you already compromise easily?

Is even thinking about working out a compromise in a discussion difficult for you? Is it your rule to never compromise?

Do not try to do all 25 questions in the same marathon session. Take the time needed to listen and be heard.

Here are some quick, simple ideas on how to approach the twenty-five probing questions in the following chapters:

One question a day will take a little less than a month to cover all 25 questions.

Make slips of paper numbered from 1 to 25. Put them in a jar or bowl. You will each pull one slip at a time out of a jar at random per session. The final session is three questions. This will take you 12 sessions to complete.

Doing one chapter at a time will take you nine sessions.

There is no question included here in this book that is off-limits for discussion. Both individuals should answer every question. No skipping the hard ones to only do the easy ones!

I grouped the questions in sections allowing you to choose where to start if my suggested format is not your priority. These sections are not necessarily in order of importance. They are compiled in this order only to help you move easily through a variety of broad relationship areas.

There is no magic scoring key at the end that you can flip to and see how compatible you are.

This is not a scored exercise.

The only scorecard is the mental one you create from a deeper understanding of how each partner feels about each answer they discuss with you.

Talk and listen to the amazing person you love with this book in hand. It is a valuable relationship-building tool.

Now it is time to get started! In chapter one, we will start with emotions and affection-related topics.

Amy Rose Herrick, ChFC
Christiansted, U.S. Virgin Islands

PDF of Questions

If you would like to print off a copy of the 25 questions mentioned in the introduction to cut apart for drawing out of a container instead of the book order format, please use one of the links below.

You will find that each question in the book has additional helpful prompts you may want to refer to when having your discussion if you use the drawing at random method.

https://www.moneywithamyaudiobooks.com/marriageafterretirementques tions

Chapter One

Emotional Questions

MONEY WITH AMY SERIES

Question #1

Do I find you affectionate to the degree I expect from my life partner?

Name_____

If yes: What do you do that makes me feel special?

If not: What do you do that does not make me feel special?

Who do you think is responsible for your happiness in our relationship?

Describe a good marriage to you.

Do you know your love language?

(Partner #2 responses begin on the next page)

Question #1 (continued)

Do I find you affectionate to the degree I expect from my life partner?

Name_____

If yes: What do you do that makes me feel special?

If not: What do you do that does not make me feel special?

Who do you think is responsible for your happiness in our relationship?

Describe a good marriage to you.

Do you know your love language?

Question #2

Do you feel I truly listen to your ideas, point of view, dreams, and complaints?

Name: _____ Yes or No

If no:

What am I doing when you feel you are not being heard, ignored, or makes you feel misunderstood?

> Interrupt you.
>
> Tune you out.
>
> Ignore you.
>
> Talk over you.
>
> Tell you what to do.

How do you react to conflict in a close relationship, giving examples?

> Do you walk away to cool off and resume the conversation later in the day, ignore the person for how long, silent treatment for how long, throw things, scream, threaten, etc.?

> Do resolution options for you include clergy or counseling with a third party, marriage retreats or others?

(Partner #2 responses begin on the next page)

Question #2 (continued)

Do you feel I truly listen to your ideas, point of view, dreams, and complaints?

Name: _____ Yes or No

If no:

What am I doing when you feel you are not being heard, ignored, or makes you feel misunderstood?

> Interrupt you.
>
> Tune you out.
>
> Ignore you.
>
> Talk over you.
>
> Tell you what to do.

How do you react to conflict in a close relationship, giving examples?

Do you walk away to cool off and resume the conversation later in the day, ignore the person for how long, silent treatment for how long, throw things, scream, threaten, etc.?

Do resolution options for you include clergy or counseling with a third party, marriage retreats or others?

Question #3

Is there any personal activity or any existing personal relationship that you expect me to give up for this relationship, including pets?

Name: _____ Yes or No

    If yes:

        Why do you expect me to give this relationship up for you?

        Am I willing to give this relationship up for you?

        Why do you expect me to give this activity up for you?

        Am I willing to give this activity up for you?

        Is there room for compromise on this subject?

        What type of pets do you expect to have in our home?

        Do you have an allergy related to pets in the home?

        Other:

(Partner #2 responses begin on the next page)

Question #3 – continued

Is there any personal activity or any existing personal relationship that you expect me to give up for this relationship, including pets?

Name: _____ Yes or No

    If yes:

      Why do you expect me to give this relationship up for you?

      Am I willing to give this relationship up for you?

      Why do you expect me to give this activity up for you?

      Am I willing to give this activity up for you?

      Is there room for compromise on this subject?

      What type of pets do you expect to have in our home?

      Do you have an allergy related to pets in the home?

    Other:

Question #4

Do you believe in, or can you see yourself being able to forgive a partner for hurtful events such as an affair, conviction of a DUI or other crime, a breach of sexual trust, a personal bankruptcy, children born out of a marriage that is not a part of your life, abortion, lying, etc.?

Name: _____ Response Yes or No

What are some examples of situations that would be so intolerable that you would end the relationship without forgiveness or compromise?

1. _____

2. _____

3. _____

(Partner #2 responses begin on the next page)

8

Question #4 continued

Do you believe in, or can you see yourself being able to forgive a partner for hurtful events such as an affair, conviction of a DUI or other crime, a breach of sexual trust, a personal bankruptcy, children born out of a marriage that is not a part of your life, abortion, lying, etc.?

Name: _____ Response Yes or No

What are some examples of situations that would be so intolerable that you would end the relationship without forgiveness or compromise?

1. _____

2. _____

3. _____

In Chapter Two, we will explore relationship questions.

Chapter Two

Relationship Questions

Question #5

Is it normal for you to snore, have a television, radio, fan, or other background noise on or bright light in the bedroom while sleeping?

Name: _____ Response Yes or No

If yes:

Do you snore?

Do you watch television in bed before falling asleep?

If you still fall asleep with the television, do you leave it on until morning?

Do you leave a radio on all night?

Do you have a fan or other appliance on all night?

Do you use any kind of sleep aid device that makes noise?

Do you require room darkening shades or drapes to block out all light to rest?

Is any noise or bright light coming through the window a problem for a light-sleeping partner?

Do you plan to sleep in the same bed with me?

What other sleep-related habits are normal for you?

(Partner #2 responses begin on the next page)

Question #5 continued

Is it normal for you to snore, have a television, radio, fan, or other background noise on or bright light in the bedroom while sleeping?

Name: _____ Response Yes or No

If yes:

Do you snore?

Do you watch television in bed before falling asleep?

If you still fall asleep with the television, do you leave it on until morning?

Do you leave a radio on all night?

Do you have a fan or other appliance on all night?

Do you use any kind of sleep aid device that makes noise?

Do you require room darkening shades or drapes to block out all light to rest?

Is any noise or bright light coming through the window a problem for a light-sleeping partner?

Do you plan to sleep in the same bed with me?

What other sleep-related habits are normal for you?

Question #6

Naming names, which of your friends, family or pets do I respect and want to spend time with, and which ones would I prefer not to spend any time with going forward?

Name: _____ Response

Persons or pets I willingly want to spend time with:

1._____

2._____

3._____

What are your relationship dynamics with these individuals?

Do not make me ever spend time with them again if I/we can figure out a way to avoid it:

1._____

2._____

3._____

What are your relationship dynamics with these individuals?

(Partner #2 responses begin on the next page)

Question #6 continued

Naming names, which of your friends, family or pets do I respect and want to spend time with, and which ones would I prefer not to spend any time with going forward?

Name: _____ Response

Persons or pets I willingly want to spend time with:

1._____

2._____

3._____

What are your relationship dynamics with these individuals?

Do not make me ever spend time with them again if I/we can figure out a way to avoid it:

1._____

2._____

3._____

What are your relationship dynamics with these individuals?

Question #7

What do you do in your free time? Am I expected or required to be a part of this activity? How much time is required?

Name: _____ Response Yes or No

     Examples:

          Reading

          Video, internet, or cell phone games

          Volunteer

          Club memberships

          Hobbies

          Exercise

          Sports activities

          Church activities

          Other

(Partner #2 responses begin on the next page)

What do you do in your free time? Am I expected or required to be a part of this activity? How much time is required?

Name_____ Response Yes or No

    Examples:

        Reading

        Video, internet, or cell phone games

        Volunteer

        Club memberships

        Hobbies

        Exercise

        Sports activities

        Church activities

        Other

In Chapter Three, we will explore medical histories and health issues.

Chapter Three
Medical Questions

Question #8

Have we fully disclosed our complete health histories and practices?

Name: _____ Response Yes or No

Examples:

Every current medication I am on for physical illness?

Every current medication I am on for mental illnesses?

Do I get yearly physicals, Pap smears, mammograms, prostate checks, bloodwork, diabetic checks, vision care, tooth cleaning, etc.?

Does Alzheimer's or any other degenerative medical condition run in my biological family?

Am I showing any early symptoms of a degenerative condition whether it has been diagnosed or not?

Have I had, or do I need any joint replacements such as knees or hips?

How serious am I about maintaining my health with regular exercise, eating habits, alcohol consumption, etc.?

Do I struggle with any type of incontinence?

Past minor and major surgeries?

Known long term medical conditions?

Suspected medical conditions?

Do you have any expected or suggested upcoming surgeries?

Any other genetic conditions that run in my family such as debilitating arthritis that would affect my ability to use my hands?

Do I have degenerative loss of vision issues that can be resolved, or will I lose my sight in time?

Do I have hearing issues that can be resolved with hearing aids if I wear them?

Do I have mobility issues now that need special equipment or that will require special equipment later?

Do I have difficulty with balance issues or navigating on my own when I need to use common elevation changing architectural features such as stairs?

Past mental illness episodes?

Drug abuse issues or history?

Alcohol abuse issues or history?

Nicotine use past or present in any form?

Do I vape?

Do I do snuff?

Domestic abuse history as victim?

Domestic abuse history as instigator?

Sexual abuse history?

Rape survivor?

Other ?

(Partner #2 responses begin on the next page)

Question #8 continued

Have we fully disclosed our complete health histories and practices?

Name: _____ Response Yes or No

Examples:

Every current medication I am on for physical illness?

Every current medication I am on for mental illnesses?

Do I get yearly physicals, Pap smears, mammograms, prostate checks, bloodwork, diabetic checks, vision care, tooth cleaning, etc.?

Does Alzheimer's or any other degenerative medical condition run in my biological family?

Am I showing any early symptoms of a degenerative condition whether it has been diagnosed or not?

Have I had, or do I need any joint replacements such as knees or hips?

How serious am I about maintaining my health with regular exercise, eating habits, alcohol consumption, etc.?

Do I struggle with any type of incontinence?

Past minor and major surgeries?

Known long term medical conditions?

Suspected medical conditions?

Do you have any expected or suggested upcoming surgeries?

Any other genetic conditions that run in my family such as debilitating arthritis that would affect my ability to use my hands?

Do I have degenerative loss of vision issues that can be resolved, or will I lose my sight in time?

Do I have hearing issues that can be resolved with hearing aids if I wear them?

Do I have mobility issues now that need special equipment or that will require special equipment later?

Do I have difficulty with balance issues or navigating on my own when I need to use common elevation changing architectural features such as stairs?

Past mental illness episodes?

Drug abuse issues or history?

Alcohol abuse issues or history?

Nicotine use past or present in any form?

Do I vape?

Do I do snuff?

Domestic abuse history as victim?

Domestic abuse history as instigator?

Sexual abuse history?

Rape survivor?

Other ?

Question #9

Do you have health, air ambulance, critical illness, cancer, disability, and/or long-term care insurance in case you become ill or injured?

Name_____ Responses Yes or No

How much of your earnings will your disability policy replace if you are still working?

Does your policy pay a fixed amount for critical illness or cancer?

How long do any systematic benefits last?

Is coverage privately owned or through your employment?

If No:

Why do you not currently have adequate health or air ambulance insurance?

What are you doing now to secure adequate health or air ambulance insurance?

Why do you not currently have disability or long-term care insurance?

What are you doing now to secure disability or long-term care insurance?

How do you plan to pay for your medical treatment without insurance?

How do you plan to meet debt and living expenses if you are injured or ill and cannot earn an income?

(Partner #2 responses begin on the next page)

Question #9 continued

Do you have health, air ambulance, critical illness, cancer, disability, and/or long-term care insurance in case you become ill or injured?

Name_____ Responses Yes or No

How much of your earnings will your disability policy replace if you are still working?

Does your policy pay a fixed amount for critical illness or cancer?

How long do any systematic benefits last?

Is coverage privately owned or through your employment?

If No:

Why do you not currently have adequate health or air ambulance insurance?

What are you doing now to secure adequate health or air ambulance insurance?

Why do you not currently have disability or long-term care insurance?

What are you doing now to secure disability or long-term care insurance?

How do you plan to pay for your medical treatment without insurance?

How do you plan to meet debt and living expenses if you are injured or ill and cannot earn an income?

In Chapter Four, we will explore financial issues that will affect your ability to maintain or accumulate wealth.

Chapter Four

Financial Questions

Question #10

Are you prepared to give up your job and/or volunteer activities to relocate with me if I am offered a career opportunity or if I want to own/rent in a location far from our present home or from either family or close friends? *Possible underlying reasoning: Perhaps you want to eliminate snow, ice accumulations, cold weather climates to reduce fall risks or you no longer want to manage substantial yard work responsibilities for health reasons in the heat.*

This household relocation could be for all or part of the calendar year.

Name: _____ Response Yes or No

If not, why not?

If yes or maybe:

> Would you only relocate to a city or metro area atmosphere?
>
> Would you be open to relocating to a rural or country atmosphere?
>
> Would you relocate outside of our current state?
>
> Would you need to secure a job before moving to a new location?
>
> Would you move to a foreign country? Temporarily for up to _____ years or less? Longer?
>
> Are you open to moving where English or _____is not the only language spoken?
>
> If we were unable to travel to see family and friends often, would this be a deal-breaker?
>
> Are you open to motorhome living on the road?
>
> Other?

(Partner #2 responses begin on the next page)

Question #10 continued

Are you prepared to give up your job and/or volunteer activities to relocate with me if I am offered a career opportunity or if I want to own/rent in a location far from our present home or from either family or close friends? *Possible underlying reasoning: Perhaps you want to eliminate snow, ice accumulations, cold weather climates to reduce fall risks or you no longer want to manage substantial yard work responsibilities for health reasons in the heat.*

This household relocation could be for all or part of the calendar year.

Name: _____ Response Yes or No

If not, why not?

If yes or maybe:

Would you only relocate to a city or metro area atmosphere?

Would you be open to relocating to a rural or country atmosphere?

Would you relocate outside of our current state?

Would you need to secure a job before moving to a new location?

Would you move to a foreign country? Temporarily for up to _____ years or less? Longer?

Are you open to moving where English or _____ is not the only language spoken?

If we were unable to travel to see family and friends often, would this be a deal-breaker?

Are you open to motorhome living on the road?

Other?

Question #11

Do you have all the estate and other legal documents current and in good order?

Examples:

General or Financial Power of Attorney (POA)?

Who is POA?	1st_____
	2nd _____
	3rd _____

Will you make any changes to this document after we are married?

Medical Power of Attorney (MPOA)

Who is POA?	1st_____
	2nd _____
	3rd _____

Will you make any changes to this document after we are married?

Will – Who is Executor

Who is listed?	1st_____
	2nd _____
	3rd _____

Will you make any changes to this document after we are married?

Living Will or Declaration

Who is listed?	1st_____
	2nd _____
	3rd _____

Will you make any changes to this document after we are married?

Revocable Living Trust

Who is Trustee? 1st_____

2nd _____

3rd _____

Will you make any changes to this document after we are married?

Irrevocable Living Trust

Who is Trustee? 1st_____

2nd _____

3rd _____

Buy/Sell agreement for any business interest owned?

Name of Business? _____

Buy/sell terms? _____

Will you make any changes to this document after we are married?

Are all property titles accurate for estate settlement?

Home _____

Vehicles _____

Boat/watercraft _____

Vacant land _____

Rental properties _____

Will you make any changes to these documents after we are married?

(Partner #2 responses begin on the next page)

Question #11 continued

Do you have all the estate and other legal documents current and in good order?

Examples:

General or Financial Power of Attorney (POA)?

Who is POA? 1st_____

2nd _____

3rd _____

Will you make any changes to this document after we are married?

Medical Power of Attorney (MPOA)

Who is POA? 1st_____

2nd _____

3rd _____

Will you make any changes to this document after we are married?

Will – Who is Executor

Who is listed? 1st_____

2nd _____

3rd _____

Will you make any changes to this document after we are married?

Living Will or Declaration

Who is listed? 1st_____

2nd _____

3rd _____

Will you make any changes to this document after we are married?

Revocable Living Trust

Who is Trustee? 1st_____

2nd _____

3rd _____

Will you make any changes to this document after we are married?

Irrevocable Living Trust

Who is Trustee? 1st_____

2nd _____

3rd _____

Buy/Sell agreement for any business interest owned?

Name of Business? _____

Buy/sell terms? _____

Will you make any changes to this document after we are married?

Are all property titles accurate for estate settlement?

Home _____

Vehicles _____

Boat/watercraft _____

Vacant land _____

Rental properties _____

Will you make any changes to these documents after we are married?

Question #12

If you needed to pay $10,000 - $100,000 for something extra or unexpected, which options would you choose to pay for it (number in order)?

Name: _____ Response

    __Get a short-term part-time job to earn the money

    __ Sell my _____ (name asset)

    __ Ask my parents/friends/relatives for the money

    __ Use money I have in savings.

            $_____ current balance.

    __ I would increase my debt load on credit cards.

            Unused credit available $_____

    __ I expect my partner to help pay for it or pay for it from their resources.

    __ Other, explain: _____

(Partner #2 responses begin on the next page)

Question #12 continued

If you needed to pay $10,000 - $100,000 for something extra or unexpected, which options would you choose to pay for it (number in order)?

Name: _____ Response

    __Get a short-term part-time job to earn the money

    __ Sell my _____ (name asset)

    __ Ask my parents/friends/relatives for the money

    __ Use money I have in savings.

            $_____ current balance.

    __ I would increase my debt load on credit cards.

            Unused credit available $_____

    __ I expect my partner to help pay for it or pay for it from their resources.

    __ Other, explain: _____

Question #13

When we get married, how do you see our family and friends being involved in our ceremony or any event following our union?

Name: _____

Examples:

Announcement

Attire of Bride, Groom and Bridal attendants

Rings

Location of ceremony

Location of Reception

Number of people to be invited

Overall budget we will not exceed $_____

Will we need to send travel money to help adult children or grandchildren attend? $_____

Honeymoon Budget $ _____

Source of funding? _____

Other _____

*If you could only afford to get married in a simple ceremony costing no more than $500-2,000 for everything with no honeymoon, no big guest list, no fancy cake, or other extras, would you still get married to me?

(Partner #2 responses begin on the next page)

When we get married, how do you see our family and friends being involved in our ceremony or any event following our union?

Name: _____

Examples:

    Announcement

    Attire of Bride, Groom and Bridal attendants

    Rings

  Location of ceremony

  Location of Reception

  Number of people to be invited

  Overall budget we will not exceed $_____

  Will we need to send travel money to help adult children or grandchildren attend? $_____

  Honeymoon Budget $ _____

  Source of funding? _____

  Other _____

*If you could only afford to get married in a simple ceremony costing no more than $500-2,000 for everything with no honeymoon, no big guest list, no fancy cake, or other extras, would you still get married to me?

Question #14

Have you disclosed to me a complete list of every financial obligation you are aware of?

Name: _____ Response Yes or No

Does this include:

All your existing debt balances including credit cards $_____

Motorcycle or car loans? $_____

Mortgage on a home, other property, or time-share? $_____

Any unpaid judgments against you? $_____

Any potential pending litigations? $_____

Student loans – current or in arrears? $_____

Child support – current or in arrears? $_____

Alimony - current or in arrears? $_____

Unpaid loans from family members? $_____

Unpaid loans from friends? $_____

Other? $_____

Tax liens or balances due on taxes from prior years?   Yes or No

Year _____ $_____

Year _____ $_____

Year _____ $_____

Total estimated debt $_____

(Partner #2 responses begin on the next page)

Question #14 continued

Have you disclosed to me a complete list of every financial obligation you are aware of?

Name: _____ Response Yes or No

Does this include:

All your existing debt balances including credit cards $_____

Motorcycle or car loans? $_____

Mortgage on a home, other property, or time-share? $_____

Any unpaid judgments against you? $_____

Any potential pending litigations? $_____

Student loans – current or in arrears? $_____

Child support – current or in arrears? $_____

Alimony - current or in arrears? $_____

Unpaid loans from family members? $_____

Unpaid loans from friends? $_____

Other? $_____

Tax liens or balances due on taxes from prior years?   Yes or No

         Year _____ $_____

         Year _____ $_____

         Year _____ $_____

Total estimated debt $_____

Question #15

Do our ideas, beliefs, and actions about life insurance, spending, and saving money for the future align perfectly or are we conducting our financial affairs now with quite different philosophies?

Name: _____ Responses

Suggestions for life insurance:

$_____gross annual earnings x 20 years   = $_____

I own $_____ of life insurance.

   Who are your current primary and contingent beneficiaries?

   Will you change your beneficiaries after we are married, or will all primary and contingent beneficiaries remain the same on existing coverage?

   Will you be securing additional life insurance with your partner as primary beneficiary?

   Why or why not?

Suggestion for disability coverage monthly earnings if still working

   $_____x 70% = $_____

   I own $_____ of disability coverage.

Suggestion for critical illness coverage annual earnings if still working.

   $_____ x 2   = $_____

   I own $_____of critical illness coverage.

Note: My suggestions for long term care coverage vary. I suggest that you consult a financial professional to coordinate needed coverage amounts to fill financial gaps combined with your resources to avoid impoverishing a surviving spouse who did not require care first.

You may want to explore a hybrid policy approach to combine life insurance and LTC benefits with in-home health care benefits or annuities that have multiple benefits for a long-term care event that may require a nursing home admission.

   $_____ X__ = $_____

   I own $_____ of coverage.

Monthly savings deposits left on deposit untouched $_____
Balance now $_____

Monthly savings for short term purchases $_____
Balance now $_____

Monthly deposits for retirement $_____
Balance now $_____

Other financial goals you are funding _____ $_____
Balance now $_____

Do you share any accounts with another person?

     Why?

     Will this change after we are married?

Will we open a new joint account or keep the finances separate?

How will we share/divide/allocate joint household expenses?

If one partner owns the home you are both living in, what will happen to the non-owner spouse's residency should the owner die?

     Legal documents will be needed.

     Life estate with what financial responsibilities?

     Move out at once?

     Inherit with an outstanding mortgage?

     Inherit with no mortgage?

     Other?

(Partner #2 responses begin on the next page)

Question #15 continued

Do our ideas, beliefs, and actions about life insurance, spending, and saving money for the future align perfectly or are we conducting our financial affairs now with quite different philosophies?

Name: _____ Responses

Suggestions for life insurance:

$_____gross annual earnings x 20 years   = $_____

I own $_____ of life insurance.

    Who are your current primary and contingent beneficiaries?

    Will you change your beneficiaries after we are married, or will all primary and contingent beneficiaries remain the same on existing coverage?

    Will you be securing additional life insurance with your partner as primary beneficiary?

    Why or why not?

Suggestion for disability coverage monthly earnings if still working

        $_____x 70% = $_____

        I own $_____ of disability coverage.

Suggestion for critical illness coverage annual earnings if still working.

        $_____ x 2   = $_____

        I own $_____of critical illness coverage.

Note: My suggestions for long term care coverage vary. I suggest that you consult a financial professional to coordinate needed coverage amounts to fill financial gaps combined with your resources to avoid impoverishing a surviving spouse who did not require care first.

You may want to explore a hybrid policy approach to combine life insurance and LTC benefits with in-home health care benefits or annuities that have multiple benefits for a long-term care event that may require a nursing home admission.

        $_____ X__ = $_____

        I own $_____ of coverage.

Monthly savings deposits left on deposit untouched $_____
Balance now $_____

Monthly savings for short term purchases $_____
Balance now $_____

Monthly deposits for retirement $_____
Balance now $_____

Other financial goals you are funding _____ $_____
Balance now $_____

Do you share any accounts with another person?

        Why?

        Will this change after we are married?

Will we open a new joint account or keep the finances separate?

How will we share/divide/allocate joint household expenses?

If one partner owns the home you are both living in, what will happen to the non-owner spouse's residency should the owner die?

        Legal documents will be needed.

        Life estate with what financial responsibilities?

        Move out at once?

        Inherit an outstanding mortgage?

        Inherit with no mortgage?

        Other?

Question #16

Before asking this question, each person must present and share a complete credit report, including their current credit score.

800 or Higher- Exceptional

740-799 Very Dependable

670-739 Good Score

580-669 Some Approved

579 and below- very Risky

Name: _____ Responses

Is your report a current accounting of your credit record? *Hint: Look on your credit card website for free access to scores.*

How and when are you going to correct any negative comments and/or repay any unpaid claims against you on the report?

Have you ever used other names or aliases? Why?

Do you qualify for credit easily now?

What is your FICO Score? _____

(Partner #2 responses begin on the next page)

Question #16 continued

Before asking this question, each person must present and share a complete credit report, including their current credit score.

800 or Higher- Exceptional

740-799 Very Dependable

670-739 Good Score

580-669 Some Approved

579 and below- very Risky

Name: _____ Responses

Is your report a current accounting of your credit record? *Hint: Look on your credit card website for free access to scores.*

How and when are you going to correct any negative comments and/or repay any unpaid claims against you on the report?

Have you ever used other names or aliases? Why?

Do you qualify for credit easily now?

What is your FICO Score? _____

Question #17

What are your sources of income, and is it enough money to work with each month to pay your expenses?

Examples:

Social Security	$_____
Pensions	$_____
Royalties	$_____
Annuity income	$_____
Contract income	$_____
Savings withdrawals	$_____
Employment	$_____
Leases	$_____
Rents collected	$_____
Other	$_____
Other	$_____

*Note: Disclose and deduct any financial support given to help other family members from income   -_____

*Note: Disclose and deduct any tithe or charity commitments given from income   -_____

Total $_____

(Partner #2 responses begin on the next page)

Question #17 continued

What are your sources of income, and is it enough money to work with each month to pay your expenses?

Examples:

Social Security $_____

Pensions $_____

Royalties $_____

Annuity income $_____

Contract income $_____

Savings withdrawals $_____

Employment $_____

Leases $_____

Rents collected $_____

Other $_____

Other $_____

*Note: Disclose and deduct any financial support given to help other family members from income   -_____

*Note: Disclose and deduct any tithe or charity commitments given from income   -_____

Total $_____

In Chapter Five, we will talk about your family related dynamics and expectations.

Chapter Five

Family Matters Questions

Question #18

Do you have children or grandchildren? Conceived in or out of marriage? Adopted?

Name: _____ Response Yes or No

If yes, be specific per child in terms of:

a) What are the names and ages of the children and grandchildren?
b) Where do they live now?
c) Where will they be living in the future?
d) What kind of child support is received or required to be paid monthly for your dependents, if any, when applies?
e) Is child support paid consistently or in arrears if applies to your minor aged dependents?
f) Have you firmly established paternity for your child dependents?
g) What are the current custody and visitation arrangements if applies?
h) Do you expect custody or visitation arrangements to change if applies?
i) Do you claim any children or grandchildren for income taxes? Every year or alternate years? Why?
j) Do you pay for health insurance for any child or grandchild? Why?
k) Do you have other support obligations related to the children or grandchildren, such as long summer vacations that you need to pay for enabling visits, annual holiday travel airfare expenses, lessons, sport activities, etc.?
l) Does your child or a grandchild have any known addiction issues such as alcohol or drug abuse?
m) Does your child or grandchild have a gambling or gaming addiction?
n) Does your child or grandchild have any mental or physical disabilities?
o) Are you helping to pay for legal issues for your children's or grandchildren's crime-related events?
p) Are you supporting any adult children or grandchildren with specific expenses or regular cash gifts?
q) How is your working relationship with the child's or grandchild's parents?
   a. Combative

b. Cooperative
c. Distance related visitation issues are a problem.
d. We have no distance related visitation issues.
e. I must go to court for issue resolution if applies.
f. We can easily converse; we are civil and attend extended family events together.
g. It is best if we are not in the same location at the same time.
h. If asked, I will help this person with anything.
i. They will die if they think I will save them.
j. They constantly ask for or demand more money.
k. I help financially when asked when I can.
l. Other.
m. Would you be willing, or are you already named as a potential guardian to raise nieces, nephews, or any grandchildren should the parent(s) die before they are adults?

(Partner #2 responses begin on the next page)

Do you have children or grandchildren? Conceived in or out of marriage? Adopted?

Name: _____ Response Yes or No

If yes, be specific per child in terms of:

a) What are the names and ages of the children and grandchildren?
b) Where do they live now?
c) Where will they be living in the future?
d) What kind of child support is received or required to be paid monthly for your dependents, if any, when applies?
e) Is child support paid consistently or in arrears if applies to your minor aged dependents?
f) Have you firmly established paternity for your child dependents?
g) What are the current custody and visitation arrangements if applies?
h) Do you expect custody or visitation arrangements to change if applies?
i) Do you claim any children or grandchildren for income taxes? Every year or alternate years? Why?
j) Do you pay for health insurance for any child or grandchild? Why?
k) Do you have other support obligations related to the children or grandchildren, such as long summer vacations that you need to pay for enabling visits, annual holiday travel airfare expenses, lessons, sport activities, etc.?
l) Does your child or a grandchild have any known addiction issues such as alcohol or drug abuse?
m) Does your child or grandchild have a gambling or gaming addiction?
n) Does your child or grandchild have any mental or physical disabilities?
o) Are you helping to pay for legal issues for your children's or grandchildren's crime-related events?
p) Are you supporting any adult children or grandchildren with specific expenses or regular cash gifts?
q) How is your working relationship with the child's or grandchild's parents?
   a. Combative

b. Cooperative
c. Distance related visitation issues are a problem.
d. We have no distance related visitation issues.
e. I must go to court for issue resolution if applies.
f. We can easily converse; we are civil and attend extended family events together.
g. It is best if we are not in the same location at the same time.
h. If asked, I will help this person with anything.
i. They will die if they think I will save them.
j. They constantly ask for or demand more money.
k. I help financially when asked when I can.
l. Other.
m. Would you be willing, or are you already named as a potential guardian to raise nieces, nephews, or any grandchildren should the parent(s) die before they are adults?

Question #19

What are your already established family holiday traditions?

As we talk about various dates, be specific in providing examples of how we could manage conflict on these days, such as:

How will we split holidays with competing invitations?

Do we have children that need time or travel to be split between households on specific days?

Do we need to plan for extra travel expenses to meet family obligations?

Can we use internet-based tools for online visits to decrease our stress levels and limit the travel required?

Name: _____ Response

Family Anniversaries _____

Family Birthdays _____

Memorial Day _____

Labor Day _____

4th of July _____

Halloween _____

Thanksgiving _____

Christmas _____

Other _____

(Partner #2 responses begin on the next page)

Question #19 continued

What are your already established family holiday traditions?

As we talk about various dates, be specific in providing examples of how we could manage conflict on these days, such as:

How will we split holidays with competing invitations?

Do we have children that need time or travel to be split between households on specific days?

Do we need to plan for extra travel expenses to meet family obligations?

Can we use internet-based tools for online visits to decrease our stress levels and limit the travel required?

Name: _____ Response

Family Anniversaries _____

Family Birthdays _____

Memorial Day _____

Labor Day _____

4th of July _____

Halloween _____

Thanksgiving _____

Christmas _____

Other _____

Question #20

Is either of us concerned about becoming a primary caregiver, guardian, or Power of Attorney for our parents, other minor-aged children in the family tree, or from close friends, or adult disabled siblings, or an incompetent family member of any age?

Name: _____ Response Yes or No

If yes:

Who is this person?

How do you envision you will need to help?

In what capacity will you need to serve his/her needs?

When do you expect this to happen?

Do you expect him/her to live with you during that time?

Will you have to move to manage this role?

Will they need to be moved to enable you to take on this role?

Will other family members share this responsibility with you?

How will any loss of income be managed if you must reduce hours or quit your job to manage the care of a loved one in need?

Do you have a Power of Attorney now for this person in your possession?

Do you have a Medical Power of Attorney for this person in your possession?

If they have a trust, are your names as a Trustee to manage trust assets when needed?

(Partner #2 responses on the next page)

Is either of us concerned about becoming a primary caregiver, guardian, or Power of Attorney for our parents, other minor-aged children in the family tree or from close friends, or adult disabled siblings, or an incompetent family member of any age?

Name: _____ Response Yes or No

If yes:

> Who is this person?
>
> How do you envision you will need to help?
>
> In what capacity will you need to serve his/her needs?
>
> When do you expect this to happen?
>
> Do you expect him/her to live with you during that time?
>
> Will you have to move to manage this role?
>
> Will they need to be moved to enable you to take on this role?
>
> Will other family members share this responsibility with you?
>
> How will any loss of income be managed if you must reduce hours or quit your job to manage the care of a loved one in need?
>
> Do you have a Power of Attorney now for this person in your possession?
>
> Do you have a Medical Power of Attorney for this person in your possession?
>
> If they have a trust, are your names as a Trustee to manage trust assets when needed?

In Chapter Six, we will explore issues that relate to your faith and religion based issues.

Chapter Six

Religious Question

Question #21

What is your plan for meeting your religious or other belief system needs?

Name: _____ Religious affiliation Yes or No

If you have a religious affiliation:

What is the name of your faith? _____

How do you visualize my part in your religious activities?

How do you visualize honoring your beliefs as a couple?

How do you visualize us honoring your beliefs in our home?

How do you visualize us honoring your beliefs if children are involved in our home?

What do you use for reference materials for your beliefs?

Would there be any reason either of us would not be accepted in a religious house of worship as a couple?

Are there specific religious traditions you plan to follow I should know about?

Do you plan to join me in my faith or religious activities if they are different from yours?

Etc.

(This discussion is continued for 2nd person on the next page)

Question #21 continued

What is your plan for meeting your religious or other belief system needs?

Name: _____ Religious affiliation Yes or No

If you have a religious affiliation:

What is the name of your faith? _____

How do you visualize my part in your religious activities?

How do you visualize honoring your beliefs as a couple?

How do you visualize us honoring your beliefs in our home?

How do you visualize us honoring your beliefs if children are involved in our home?

What do you use for reference materials for your beliefs?

Would there be any reason either of us would not be accepted in a religious house of worship as a couple?

Are there specific religious traditions you plan to follow I should know about?

Do you plan to join me in my faith or religious activities if they are different from yours?

Etc.

In Chapter Seven, we will explore issues that relate to your new household needs and management of day-to-day tasks.

Chapter Seven

Household Management Question

MONEY WITH AMY SERIES

Question #22

Describe your expectations for household management.

Name: _____ Responses

Examples:

What is your expectation of any gender or title related roles in our household such as wife/husband/partner?

Who do you envision doing the following?

Washing dishes

Cooking meals

Laundry

Vacuuming and sweeping floors

Pet care, including food, grooming and vet visits etc.

How much dust or clutter is acceptable to you?

Are you physically able to do heavy work like lifting furniture, lawn work, or other home maintenance items, or must these be hired out?

Is homeownership important to you?

Who manages landscaping and lawn type care?

Pool care?

Do you clean your own home, or do you have maid services?

How often should the floor be mopped?

How often should the shower be cleaned?

How often should the sheets on the bed be changed?

Other:

(Partner #2 responses begin on the next page)

Question #22 continued

Describe your expectations for household management.

Name: _____ Responses

Examples:

What is your expectation of any gender or title related roles in our household such as wife/husband/partner?

Who do you envision doing the following?

Washing dishes

Cooking meals

Laundry

Vacuuming and sweeping floors

Pet care, including food, grooming and vet visits etc.

How much dust or clutter is acceptable to you?

Are you physically able to do heavy work like lifting furniture, lawn work, or other home maintenance items, or must these be hired out?

Is homeownership important to you?

Who manages landscaping and lawn type care?

Pool care?

Do you clean your own home, or do you have maid services?

How often should the floor be mopped?

How often should the shower be cleaned?

How often should the sheets on the bed be changed?

Other:

Question #23

Describe your expectations and financial plans for how you will be cared for if you become physically or mentally disabled.

Name: _____ Responses

Examples:

Where will you be living if you need only minimal support?

If at home, who will provide your care there?

Do you intend to move in with a family member?

Have they agreed to this?

Would I, as your spouse, be welcome there too?

How will you/we pay for this change?

Will you move to a facility when you need a higher level of care?

Where?

How will you/we pay for it?

Will I be able to stay in our family home for my lifetime if I do not need the same level of care and I can live independently?

(Partner #2 responses on the next page)

Question #23 continued

Describe your expectations and financial plans for how you will be cared for if you become physically or mentally disabled.

Name: _____ Responses

Examples:

Where will you be living if you need only minimal support?

If at home, who will provide your care there?

Do you intend to move in with a family member?

Have they agreed to this?

Would I, as your spouse, be welcome there too?

How will you/we pay for this change?

Will you move to a facility when you need a higher level of care?

Where?

How will you/we pay for it?

Will I be able to stay in our family home for my lifetime if I do not need the same level of care and I can live independently?

In Chapter Eight, we will feel perhaps a little uneasy or vulnerable as we discuss our sexuality expectations and preferences.

Chapter Eight
Sexuality Question

MONEY WITH AMY SERIES

Question #24

Have you had one or more sexual partners before me, and do you have specific sexual expectations to be met in our future?

Name: _____ Response Yes or No

If yes:

> How many?
>
> Do your sexual experiences include more than one sexual orientation?
>
> Did you contract any sexual disease in a prior relationship?
>
> Do you have current AIDS, HIV, STD testing results to share with me?
>
> > If not, are you willing to obtain AID, HIV or other STD testing and share your certificate of health results with me?
>
> Can I comfortably and openly discuss sexual needs, preferences, dislikes, and fears inside and outside of the bedroom citing specific examples of likes and dislikes?
>
> What frequency is a healthy sex life to you weekly/monthly?
>
> Are there any sexual expectations after marriage for the inclusion of sex toys, swinging, other partners etc.?
>
> What are your personal hygiene practices or expectations before or after sex?
>
> Other?

(Partner #2 responses begin on the next page)

Have you had one or more sexual partners before me, and do you have specific sexual expectations to be met in our future?

Name: _____ Response Yes or No

If yes:

How many?

Do your sexual experiences include more than one sexual orientation?

Did you contract any sexual disease in a prior relationship?

Do you have current AIDS, HIV, STD testing results to share with me?

If not, are you willing to obtain AID, HIV or other STD testing and share your certificate of health results with me?

Can I comfortably and openly discuss sexual needs, preferences, dislikes, and fears inside and outside of the bedroom citing specific examples of likes and dislikes?

What frequency is a healthy sex life to you weekly/monthly?

Are there any sexual expectations after marriage for the inclusion of sex toys, swinging, other partners etc.?

What are your personal hygiene practices or expectations before or after sex?

Other?

In our final Chapter Nine, we will discuss whether a prenuptial agreement will be completed with the help of separate legal counsel.

Chapter Nine
Prenuptial Question

MONEY WITH AMY SERIES

Question #25

Does either of us expect to engage an attorney to draw up and formally implement a prenuptial agreement before we are married?

Name: _____ Response Yes or No

If yes, what are some things we are thinking about:

Comingling our household obligations?

Commingling our assets?

Commingling our income resources?

Filing taxes as a couple for joint tax liability or filing separately for individual liability?

> *Hint: Check current local jurisdiction and Federal laws for any* specific requirements?

Commingling future joint debt?

Who will pay ongoing household expenses?

How will housing be owned?

How will vehicles be owned?

How will other property be owned?

Inheritances for any children born or adopted prior to this union will be _____

Inheritances for any children born or adopted in this union (when applies) will be _____

Life estate in real estate owned by only one spouse.

Will you set up a Revocable Living Trust?

Will you set up an Irrevocable Living trust?

Will you sell one home and invest any proceeds in a different home? How will this be managed for estate planning?

Other?

(This discussion is continued for 2nd person on the next page)

Question #25 continued

Does either of us expect to engage an attorney to draw up and formally implement a prenuptial agreement before we are married?

Name: _____ Response Yes or No

If yes, what are some things we are thinking about:

Comingling our household obligations?

Commingling our assets?

Commingling our income resources?

Filing taxes as a couple for joint tax liability or filing separately for individual liability?

Hint: Check current local jurisdiction and Federal laws for any specific requirements.

Commingling future joint debts?

Who will pay ongoing household expenses?

How will housing be owned?

How will vehicles be owned?

How will other property be owned?

Inheritances for any children born or adopted prior to this union will be _____

Inheritances for any children born or adopted in this union (when applies) will be _____

Life estate in real estate owned by only one spouse.

Will you set up a Revocable Living Trust?

Will you set up an Irrevocable Living trust?

Will you sell one home and invest any proceeds in a different home? How will this be managed for estate planning?

Other?

Afterthoughts: We have a big problem. We are at an impasse.

Some of you may be hurt by a revelation because of the probing or deeply personal questions asked.

Perhaps you found you have quite different ideas on a topic you had assumed you would be compatible with.

Whatever happened, you feel stuck on a divisive issue or two, and now what should you do?

You should go to the next step to seek a qualified, trusted resource to help you further discuss the issue to see where you can compromise and where you cannot.

Not agreeing on everything is not always a relationship-ending event, but it could be if it is a non-negotiable item for either partner.

You could seek help from a pastor, priest, or other clergy member. Perhaps you choose a professional counselor, psychologist, medical professional, or other qualified people who can help give you more clarity or insight may be helpful. You are not right or wrong to feel the way you do about any issue. It is a part of who you are.

Who can help answer your questions, address your fears of the unknown or help you to understand the other person's perspective better?

Who can help you reach a compromise?

In some situations, you may ultimately decide to let this relationship go if you cannot see a future together as being the one you seek. Who will be your support system?

Not addressing the issue that is threatening your future happiness is not a solution. It is generally an unwise decision to ignore something. Ignoring an issue is often called "the elephant in the room" syndrome. Avoiding mentioning the elephant like it will suddenly disappear is different from trying to find a solution before the elephant takes over everything and everyone's attention in the whole house.

I wish you the best of times as you invest so much of your future into each other. Congratulations on knowing your chosen partner better than ever before.

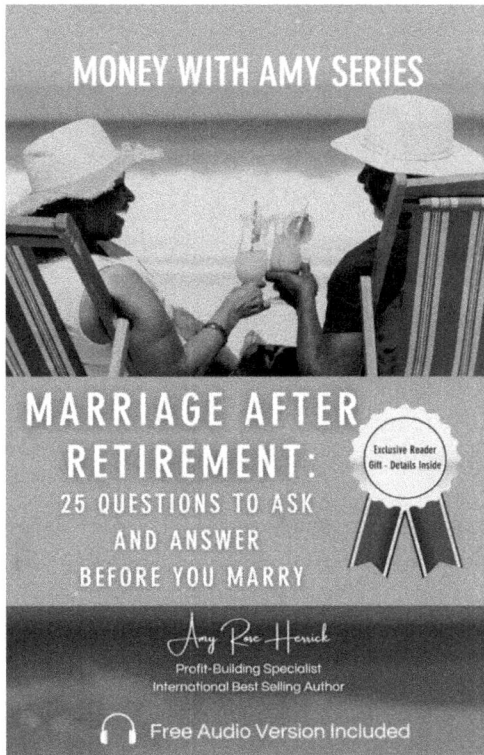

THANK YOU FOR READING MY BOOK!

As a thank-you, we'd love to send you a free bonus book- not for sale anywhere else. Just email us at INFO@AmyRoseHerrick.com with "Bonus Book Request" in the subject line. You'll receive your exclusive gift directly by email.

Loved the book? We'd be grateful for your honest review on Amazon— but the bonus is yours either way.

ACKNOWLEDGMENTS

Without the support of many over the years, I could not be the person I am today. I know I will forget to thank someone, but it was not my intention to do so.

To my family, who do not always understand me, but love me anyway, you mean the world to me.

To friends and colleagues who support my professional talents and literary dreams, I wish you continued success in your endeavors.

To my talented VA team who helped me to have the finished content in print form, may your dreams come true too.

To the online writing groups from around the world on Zoom meetings where we encouraged each other in the manuscript writing processes, I did it and so can you!

To my clients and live audiences who helped me learn so much about this topic with the sharing of their life stories of successes and failures for me to give guidance to you today, thank you for allowing me to have a positive impact on your lives.

To my mentors, I promise to pay it forward.

To my draft version reviewers with all the helpful suggestions and encouragement to get this finished quickly, you will see many of your suggestions incorporated.

And finally, to all the ones behind the scenes we take for granted that make websites, online ordering, eBooks, printing, shipping, and delivery possible for us all...a heartfelt thank you for being a part of my world every day.

About the Author

Amy Rose Herrick, ChFC, is an extraordinary author and financial expert dedicated to transforming lives while empowering individuals and businesses to achieve unparalleled financial success.

Some remarkable solutions take 15 minutes or less to understand and implement.

Her expertise shines brightest creating personalized, comprehensive plans that streamline costs, provide peace of mind, and secure wealth for future generations.

Bid farewell to financial stress while embracing your legacy that will endure the test of time.

Amy, your personal wealth building guide, unleashes the power within your resources.

Complex resource management problems are transformed into easy step by step solutions.

Using groundbreaking methodology, Amy empowers individuals, business owners, and families alike.

Entrepreneurs flock to Amy for clear, actionable tutorials on building more profitable businesses. Under her guidance, ventures can thrive like never before, unlocking their true potential for financial success.

As a fiduciary, Chartered Financial Consultant, and tax professional, Amy has mastered the art of optimizing resources.

Yet, her achievements do not stop there. She is a #1 Best Selling Author, captivating speaker, talented artist, and a dedicated force in community service.

With over three decades of experience, including more than 25 years in the Securities industry, Amy possesses an impressive array of qualifications and expertise. She equips you with the tools to experience lasting financial freedom, providing a transformative journey unlike any other.

In 2024, be prepared for the launch of a series of game-changing books and captivating YouTube videos titled "Money With Amy."

Her dynamic and easy-to-understand content will empower you to strategically structure your resources for the benefit of your family and businesses.

Amy Rose Herrick's list of remarkable accomplishments is truly awe-inspiring. From being named Small Business of the Year to being a #1 Best Selling Author, a National Geographic 'Chasing Genius' Finalist, and even teaching a gorilla named Max, Amy's impact is undeniable.

Clients can expect an unforgettable, life-changing experience with Amy Rose Herrick, one that simply cannot be replicated elsewhere.

Currently residing by the sea in the breathtaking US Virgin Islands, Amy continues to live a life of abundance while sharing her wealth of knowledge with the world.

For Additional Information & Resources

Visit Amy's website: **www.AmyRoseHerrick.com**

Email: **Amy@AmyRoseHerrick.com**

Book a 15-minute Zoom based discovery call to discuss becoming a client for comprehensive financial planning or business profit building assistance at:

https://calendly.com/amyroseherrick/15min

Follow Amy on Facebook

https://www.facebook.com/AmyRoseHerrickProfitBuildingSpecialist

Listen to several Podcast appearances on a variety of topics:

https://www.listennotes.com/search/?q=amy%20rose%20herrick&sort_by_date=0&scope=episode&offset=0&language=Any%20language&len_min=0

Read Amy's articles on Medium at :
https://medium.com/search?q=amy+rose+herrick

Reach out to Amy at Amy@AmyRoseHerrick.com to inquire about booking Amy to be on your show as a guest or for autographed copies.

Watch one of Amy's full length financial literacy building educational videos on YouTube

https://www.youtube.com/@amyprofitspecialist

Linked in: https://www.linkedin.com/in/amyroseherrick/

Instagram: amyroseherrick

Alignable: https://www.alignable.com/christiansted-vi/amy-rose-herrick-chfc-americas-profit-building-specialist

Amazon all current titles for sale link:

https://www.amazon.com/s?k=amy+rose+herrick&crid=SGL1PHGTWZS5&sprefix=amy+rose+herrick%2Caps%2C179&ref=nb_sb_noss_1

Other titles available now, or coming soon, in the MONEY WITH AMY SERIES that may be of interest to you:

MONEY WITH AMY SERIES

Protecting Your Health and Wealth:
Your Step-by-Step Guide for
Multi-Generational Medical
Planning

Exclusive Reader
Gift - Details Inside

Amy Rose Herrick
Profit-Building Specialist
International Best Selling Author

Free Audio Version Included

MONEY WITH AMY SERIES

HOW TO IDENTIFY
A QUALIFIED
ADVISOR

Exclusive Reader
Gift - Details Inside

Amy Rose Herrick
Profit-Building Specialist
International Best Selling Author

MONEY WITH AMY SERIES

Building your
foundation:
ENTREPRENEURIAL
MISTAKES TO AVOID

Exclusive Reader
Gift - Details Inside

Amy Rose Herrick
Profit-Building Specialist
International Best Selling Author

Free Audio Version Included

MONEY WITH AMY SERIES

KNOWING YOUR LIFE PARTNER:

25 QUESTIONS TO ASK AND ANSWER (FOR COUPLES IN THEIR FIRST LONG TERM RELATIONSHIP)

Exclusive Reader Gift - Details Inside

Amy Rose Herrick

Profit-Building Specialist
International Best Selling Author

Free Audio Version Included

MONEY WITH AMY SERIES

REMARRIAGE:

Exclusive Reader
Gift - Details Inside

25 QUESTIONS TO ASK
AND ANSWER
BEFORE REMARRIAGE

Amy Rose Herrick

Profit-Building Specialist
International Best Selling Author

🎧 Free Audio Version Included

Self-Employed Taxes:

Unleashing Schedule C Deductions A Line-By-Line Guide to Unlock Deductions and Create New Tax Savings for Small Business Owners and Independent Contractors

Exclusive Reader Gift - Details Inside

Amy Rose Herrick

Profit-Building Specialist
International Best Selling Author

🎧 Free Audio Version Included

MONEY WITH AMY SERIES

The Profitable Entrepreneur:

16 Ways to Retrain Entrepreneurs Using Mindset, Time Management, Leveraging Your Resources and Enjoying More Business Travel Inexpensively

Exclusive Reader Gift - Details Inside

Amy Rose Herrick

Profit-Building Specialist
International Best Selling Author

Free Audio Version Included

www.ingramcontent.com/pod-product-compliance
Lightning Source LLC
Chambersburg PA
CBHW060250030426
42335CB00014B/1646